GW01269945

HOME IS NEITHER HERE NOR THERE

Nandi Jola

Doire Press

First published in 2022

Doire Press
Aille, Inverin
Co. Galway
www.doirepress.com

Layout: Lisa Frank
Cover design: Tríona Walsh
Cover art: agsandrew @ Shutterstock.com
Author photo: Maciek Bator

Printed by Clódóirí CL
Casla, Co. na Gaillimhe

Copyright © Nandi Jola

ISBN 978-1-907682-89-6

All rights reserved. No part of this publication may be reproduced or transmitted in any form or by any means. This book is sold subject to the usual trade conditions.

We gratefully acknowledge the assistance of The Arts Council of Northern Ireland.

LOTTERY FUNDED

CONTENTS

About the Author	9

I: The Journey (Inye: Uhambo)

My Soul	10
Journey of the Magi	11
Somewhere between Belfast and Africa	12
Identity	13
Peace Walls (Belfast)	14
I am a Xhosa	15
Hair	16
Ink	17
Arrivals	18
Messenger of the Gods	19

II: Home (Zimbini: Ikhaya)

Mother	20
Still	21
Umzi Watsha	22

Looked-After Children	23
Absent Daughter	24
Police Interview Redacted	25
Tape 1	
Tape 2	
Tape 3	
Tape 4	
Tape 5	
Pictures of the Place	27

III: Demise *(Zintathu: Ukufa)*

Resistance	28
Great House	29
Brussels (Will Fix Me)	30
Let Us In	31
Irish Pilgrimage	32
Strange Fruit	33

Nongqhawuse	34
Freak Show	35
Red Light	36
Sarah's Cake	37
Brainless Skull	38

IV: The State of Us (Zine: Imeko Yethu)

I'm Not a Racist, But	39
You Weren't Born Here, Were You?	40
Can I Touch Your Hair?	41
Did You Come Here by Boat?	42
Irish People Were Slaves Too	43
Black Irish	44

V: Apartheid (Zintlanu: Ucalucalulo)

Sharpeville Massacre	45
Unsung	46

June 16, 1976	47
Legacy	48
Thula Mama Thula	49
Senzeni Na (What Have We Done)?	50
46664	51
Dunnes Stores' Workers (Dublin)	52
Never, Never and Never Again	53
Memory Unexpurgated	54

VI: Love (Zintandathu: Uthando)

Entomology	55
Tapestry of Love	56

VII: Veranda Sunsets (Zisixhenxe: Ukutshona Kwelanga Kwiveranda) — 57

Acknowledgements	62
About the Author	63

For Anesu Khanya — my Black Irish child

About the Author

Black
Middle child
First of her family to emigrate
Left South Africa for Northern Ireland which she had never heard of
Spent five years trying to live the dream by working an office job
The following fifteen spent discovering and reinventing herself
Classical music her first love
Always wished to speak Irish to add to Xhosa fluency
Owns too many shoes
Sometimes words don't always come out the way she thinks them
Needs auto-correct all the time

I: The Journey (Inye: Uhambo)

My Soul

An African child strives in the basking heat
her hair is like silk
her skin is the most beautiful treasure
she is majestic
regal
tall
her teeth so white
she is a poem
the poem in the Songs of Solomon.

Journey of the Magi

I likened my plane journey to the journey told by T.S. Eliot
in his poem 'Journey of the Magi'
where the wise men stopped
got drunk
fought
nearly lost the gifts.
We like to believe that this journey was the holy of holies,
but it was mayhem
these men were far from wise
they travelled from the old to the new
in search of a Baby, they thought.
And now I was travelling from the old to the new world
in search of
I didn't know then
and to be honest I still don't know now
I only knew the name of my destination was a place called
Belfast.

Somewhere between Africa and Belfast

are broken promises
rain
brown soil
God
friendship
love
Madiba on the Peace Wall
and pain
bullet pain
riot pain
death
life
history.

Identity

I am too white to be black
I am too black to be white
not a Catholic neither a Protestant
a new thing
something Ireland didn't have fifty years ago
a sin
a coconut
human.

Peace Walls (Belfast)

I come from teargas
necklace
dompass
toy-toy
kill the Boer
kaffir
we stood in defiance
we conquered
no peace walls there.

I am a Xhosa

Amaxhosa are storytellers
kwasekuqaleni
from the beginning
nasekugqibeleni
till the end
camagu
Amen
cingcilili
forevermore.

Hair

Not a day goes by without someone touching me
my hair
is my body
more hands
in my hair
I am not tan
dark-skinned
coloured
I am Black
Black as Angela Davis
as slavery
like Apartheid
history
struggle
Black
my hair, my flag
my roots
my decolonisation
confidence
you would rather I cover it up
straighten it
curl it
put a wig over it
weave it
no
it demands to be seen
it commands it
it is iconic
symbolic
it is me
my hair.

Ink

A letter came today
ten years late, but it arrived
majestic and reverent
it addressed me by my first name
with titles Miss and Dear

The letter came today
ten years late, but it arrived
I am now a Citizen
I will breathe the same air as you
walk the streets of Belfast without fear
roam Ireland like a bird
I am no longer a case number
a statistic
I'm not on the next charter plane
nor am I going from detention to deportation
I am free
the letter came.

Arrivals

We came in our rags
with smiles and full of hope
unpacked into our matchbox homes
in places called Springfarm
with pictures of our exotic places and things fixed on the walls
then, we ventured out to the reality
through interfaces we crossed
called foreigners
sometimes welcomed
not mentioning our religion
our gods
we danced
we sang
in our gay clothes
selling our culture
waking the bones of this troubled City.

Messenger of the Gods

The flickering clicks
breaks the quiet
lighting the pipe
ritual
her lungs contract and expand
like bagpipes
you sniff it first,
down it,
then it gets to your head
and just then you transcend
between dreams.

II: Home (Zimbini: Ikhaya)

Mother

Our house always looked sterile just like Mother
it had clear distinction of dos and don'ts
mother, a teacher
comes from a wealthy family and she always reminded us
me and my brother
that eating garlic and avocados was not a white people thing.

Still

He looks at himself
in the mirror
holding a photo
taken in 1983
thinking,
if only I never hit my wife
I never hit my children.

Umzi Watsha

I watched her unpack dad's belongings
one by one
they disappeared
out of sight
the elephant tusk paraffin lamp
bought in Swaziland in 1980
the straw hat from Lesotho
his brown leather belt with a silver buckle
that he used to beat us up with

umzi watsha umzi watsha
khangela phaya
khangela phaya
umlilo umlilo
galelamanzi galelamanzi

I only learnt later that this was a French rhyme
'Frère Jacques'
to mock
to taunt
us, Africans
we sang it to cheer a man
for beating up his wife
we sang it whilst playing with paper dolls
banging them together.

Looked-After Children

On my last review
I screamed like a wild boar
'She is my child'
no one can braid her hair like I do
or fry plantain and cook okra
sing my native songs
and teach her poetry
'I am her mother'
I'm reclaiming her
she is mine
that's how I got her back
in my arms again.

Absent Daughter

I always buy her expensive perfume
designer bags
beautiful clothes from Marks and Spencer
she always brags to her sisters
I say nothing
I go back to charity shops for these finds.

Mother on the other hand
has only met her granddaughter twice in ten years
once when she was two
then when she just turned twelve
she never tries to ring her
Irish accent in a Brown skin
is not something she gets
as if we are talking about another gift
then again that's all she is used to
not relationships.

Police Interview Redacted

Tape 1
Is there anything you are not telling us?
No
Are you sure?
Yes
You know that perpetrators don't change their behaviour right?
Silence...

Tape 2
You don't have to go back
that is my house
are things that bad?
I worked three jobs to buy that house in Maghaberry
tell me I'm not going to have to sell it
tell me you can keep him away
tell me this will not ruin my chances of getting Citizenship

Tape 3
You speak good English
you must be well-educated
which country do you come from?
don't worry we will find you a place to stay for tonight
a safe place
they will help you there
at least you drive
you must be exhausted, pet
is it a girl or a boy?
she is gorgeous
what do you call her?
beautiful name.

Tape 4
Women's Refuge
your status says no recourse to public funds
that means you can't stay here
you are not entitled to benefits
I can't work until I renew my visa
he won't sign the paperwork
I rang the housing and they said
I can sleep in the car with my two-year-old
and I did.

Tape 5
I was told I can't be helped
we are going to take the child into care
we are concerned for her safety
what does that mean?
she will be looked after by a foster family
whilst you try and find help
when will I get her back?
when social services are satisfied
that it is safe for her to return to you.

Pictures of the Place

I used to wait on the edge of the window
each day for my child to come flying down the road,
her face filled with a smile
and the promise of things to come.
The days were longer then.
The summers when there were kids everywhere,
the neighbours kept their doors open and the calls to
come play were constant.
Bring back those days of cartoons on the telly,
alphabet potatoes and dilute juice,
ice pops and curly crisps,

when chicken nuggets and chips were golden
and 10p mixups were a treat.
Bring back the milkman,
the sound of the ice cream van,
the sound of children playing in the fields,
trees where the birds perched and returned each year.
Bring back my dreams of the things that never were
and those flowers that never came back.

III: Demise (Zintathu: Ukufa)

Resistance

I see you
the tear on your brow
hips full of swing
gaps between your teeth
you come year after year
to this Pilgrimage
lining the streets of Belfast
then the chant starts
the drum beat
one two, one two
your feet begin to twitch
like child soldiers
gasping
days like this will return
like a bird song
once mother nature awakens
so will our grasp.

Great House

That night the lamp was burning low
beasts arranged, rounded up and counted
by the kraal, wood pilled and dried for days
windows adorned in their bewailing clothes
the elders in shrouds.

A woman entered the Royal House
from the stoep towards the veranda
with a balm in her hand
and a white cloth around her torso.

From a distance six men approached
with shovels on their shoulders
through the mist
passing the beasts
and the wood
to the other side they walked
alluding to Augusta Savage's work.

Brussels (Will Fix Me)

She pierced through my virginity
blade on one hand
other stroking my cornrowed hair
I wet myself
blood gushing down my tender thighs
he looks at me as a husband does
I look at him intimately
I feel nothing
he speaks
not even the scent of rose water
or pomegranate perfume I bathed in
I can't make him stay
Brussels is where they stitch girls like me
fix me.

Let Us In

She dances in the wind
her feet barely touch the ground
hair like an evening sunset
whispers to her heart
her silhouette echoes a sense of presence
still lingering in the silent and empty streets
we search within our souls for a witness
an ear, so we can hear her screams
as she is silenced by unyielding hands
we want to feel your pain
your last draw of breath
the drop of your earring
twisting of your necklace
your heart's last beat
so you don't go through this alone
let us in.

Irish Pilgrimage

The most silent of places
is a valley
on the cliff
in it
a rock dripping
holy water.

The rock has succumbed
to the power of the water.

Only a few mountain goats
brave the winters there
and some foliage too
the ground is covered
by a white blanket
underneath, the turf breathes.

I stumbled upon this place
I took my shoes off
then bowed
lifting my hands
poured my soul out.

Nature has a way
of
enveloping us back to it.

Strange Fruit

We
are worse than animals
lower than snake's ass
even the darkness still offers light
but we, we
slumber
drown
in the stagnant waters
of our parallels.

Nongqawuse

I believe you
they lied
men lie
they rape
women get blamed
even in 1891.

Freak Show

How do you imagine the Houses of Parliament
in the 1800s Britain?
Did you foretell a freak show?
a trafficked woman exhibited.
Naked
touched
her buttocks an amusement?
Caged
men with cigars
women wearing wigs
laughing to their heart's content?
England, I hate you
South Africa
was her home
now, her soul is caged here
in these chambers.

Red Light

Think how a woman was bought
trafficked
sold again

South Africa
to England
then France
over to Sweden

a scientific experiment in the end.

Sarah's Cake

Clitoridectomy
voluptuous
Hottentot Venus
this is a cake
mocking
no repenting.

Sweden.

Brainless Skull

Her body parts were finally returned
Britain, breasts
France, buttocks
Sweden, face
Where is her brain?
Who has kept her wisdom?

IV: The State of Us (Zine: Imeko Yethu)

I'm Not a Racist, But

I know
you are simply asking why
so many people want to come here
to take your jobs, your houses
when you have given so much to them
a penny every Sunday in Church
at the corner shop in the Trócaire box
with the Black baby
them a penny, gold for you in return
keep digging diamonds
I keep a penny for you
sweet sugar, a penny
coffee too, another penny
so, you are not a racist
I hear you.

You Weren't Born Here, Were You?

Anyone who is different cannot be interwoven
between us and them
in the orange and green
of our culture
our fabric cannot be dyed
nor can family cross be remade
we will invent boxes instead
Black Irish
Black other.

Can I Touch Your Hair?

The same hair Black people were forced to cut, cover up
to erase their culture
identity
tribe
the same hair that Blacks braided
as cornrows to map an escape route on their heads
from the plantation
escaping slavery
the same hair they would hide rice or grain in
so that their children ate, in case they were sent to the Black
Friday market
to be sold to the next master
the same hair that the ancestors prayed over
today I wear it as a crown
a symbol of resilience
you want to touch it?
How about you learn about Black Friday first?

Did You Come Here by Boat?

No
a Black woman invented navigation in the 20th century
Gladys Mae West
born 1930
a mathematician, she worked
on the mathematical modelling of the shape of the earth
and on the development of the satellite global positioning system
so I can fly
it was White men that travelled by boat to Africa,
remember that.

Irish People Were Slaves Too

Did they work in the plantations
picking cotton for over four hundred years?
were they lynched as well?
burnt at the stake?
segregated
sold
do they have a need to say Irish Lives Matter today?

Black Irish

We met at sea
in Cape Agulhas
the infinite world
running in confluence.

Eight *ante meridiem*
a boy on a bus no.11
translates to his Mother
like a needle on a thread
weaving in and our
of English and Swahili.

A nun taps the woman on the shoulder
habari
habari yako?
hello
how are you?
then they speak for the rest of the journey
through their habit and hijab.

The boy's limb stretches towards the bell
between prams, stairs and moist breath of an early bus
she struts and below under pale faces
to the halt of the bus.

This is what Irish means
she thinks to herself
strangers speaking to you in Swahili
a child that thinks his Father was from the Falls.

V: Apartheid (Zintlanu: Ucalucalulo)

Sharpeville Massacre

He steps out
holding his Dompass
then he shouts
enough is enough
he senses the tension
he smells the burning tyres
oblivious to his last steps
his last breath
freedom
he takes a milestone
approaching history
this hero
whose name we don't know
will always be remembered

They open fire
5,000 to 7,000 people
screams
shot in the back
gasping
lifeless
eyes wide open
69
bubbling blood clots
mark each spot.

Unsung

Wives raising children
men in prison
46664
Robben Island
watch their children go up in flames
necklace
tortured
whipped
kicked
bruised
Bantu Biko.

June 16, 1976

Orlando Stadium
Vilakazi Street
on the corner of Moema Street
Hector Pieterson
no smell of gunpowder
dogs started to bark
then footsteps
screaming children
he says, 'futsek'.

Legacy

They said to leave stones unturned
for trees to keep their roots
moss returns every winter turning into a purple blanket
sky, orange, blue with a hymn of the birds.

The click of milk bottles
sharpness of coal burning aroma
expanding your lungs to take a breath
hope.

It is the bones of those who died on SS Mendi that brought me here
Sarah Baartman called me
Mandela Hall
for is it here that Mandela became an icon
in Belfast
a visionary

Tata, I am here.

Thula Mama Thula

Thula
Peace
Thula Mama thula
Peace Mama Peace
Thula Mama thula
Peace Mama Peace
Black woman is the most disrespected person
Black woman is the most unprotected person
she has raised white boys as her own
suckled them
Thula
Peace.

Senzeni Na (What Have We Done)?

Captured
chained
whipped
sold
picking cotton
segregated
burnt
lynched
shot
jailed
assassinated.

46664

Open seas of
Robben Island
opened the eyes
of the world
opened the doors
to freedom.

Dunnes Stores' Workers (Dublin)

In solidarity you stood for us.
yanga imisebenzi yezandla zenu
may the work of your hands
ingacimeki ezingqondweni
be never erased from our minds
nasemiphefumlweni yethu
from our spirits
kude kube ngonaphakade
until eternity
Enkosi
Thank you.

'Never, Never and Never Again'

Never again shall I be called a 'Kaffir'
never again will my children be segregated
in the land of their ancestors
never again will I speak Afrikaans
isiXhosa is my language
in my land, South Africa, I shall walk free carrying no Dom Pass
Vilakazi Street
in 1976 June 16
you were covered in blood
at number1185 Vilakazi Street

Noble man
Everlasting Hero
Lion of Peace
Son of Africa
Obedient
National Treasure

Rholihlahla Mandela is his name
May 1994 Union Buildings Pretoria
Peace and Reconciliation were your words
Ubuntu you proclaimed
forgiveness you pleaded
a rainbow nation you gave birth to
and in your words… **'Never, never and never again.'**

Memory Unexpurgated

The days
were not
always
filled with
tear gas
and burning flesh
but
laugher too
and the smell
of
homemade bread.

VI: Love *(Zintandathu: Uthando)*

Entomology

Our bodies are wiretaps
carried by a cuboid vessel
into the viscera of sphere
like weevils bare to illumination
leaning on the nearest thing
the thing that is itinerant
of the two dimensions
at the speed of light
transporting us through
quotidian noise.

Tapestry of Love

Let us give Love a chance
to give our children hope
of a world without hatred
where Black and White walk hand in hand
let the peace walls come down
for the ghosts of troubles to be finally laid to rest
for history to remain history
only to be found in books on shelves
stories must be told by those that are victorious
together let us dance to freedom
emancipate to one song
one love
for we are one race
of many colours
many voices
many dreams
one unity
one heart
a tapestry of love.

VII: Veranda Sunsets (Zisixhenxe: Ukutshona Kwelanga Kwiveranda)

Our house always looked sterile, just like mother. It had a clear divide of dos and don'ts. Mother, a teacher, comes from a wealthy family and she always reminded us, me and my brother, that using a knife and fork at the table was manners, and not a white people thing or colonisation, but my father's side thought we were brought up white.

Following her ways of doing things was like walking on eggshells, not knowing when next the insult would come. She looked at us as if we stopped time, as if she was frozen in time, like she was trapped in an hourglass. In fact, she reminded us all the time that before we arrived on this planet, there was no Apartheid, as if we brought it with us on our arrival. Like when babies carry their food in their umbilical cords from wherever they came from, Pluto or Mars, I don't know. She gently recalls in her soft voice 'the good old days', as she calls them.

I tiptoed into the kitchen in my new pyjamas, the sizzling bacon, eggs and fresh toast filling the house. 'Morning,' I said. My voice met with silence. I kind of muddled around to reach the kettle on the other side, avoiding any eye contact. Her voice was drowning in the aroma, but I could still make out that she was singing a hymn 'Lizalise idinga lakho Thixo Nkosi Wenyaniso', deep in thought and far removed from the pan she was meant to be stirring. The apron just hanging on her exhausted body on what was meant to be breasts, her freckled face now just bowed down in prayer and her eyes shed a tear or two.

I eventually reached the kettle and just tapped the switch. That brought her back to the moment again, and then I asked her 'tea or coffee?'

She looked at me and we gasped at each other. It was rare to see her cry. I can count on one hand when that occurred and I don't think she liked me witnessing that side of her. Just when we were at the mercy of each other's gaze, my little brother, Stan, walked in with his big feet slapping across the white ceramic tiled floor, he just cut us off like the way we used to have blackouts in the 1980s. All that heat in the kitchen diffused. The glare, the connection, the cooking, it all stopped simultaneously, and we all ate there with our knives and folks in silence, blacked-out just wondering what to say.

Then, I asked about my grandfather, with my innocent and curious tone, waiting for an honest answer as she always gave to us. Brutal, sharp, she looked me in the eye and said, 'He disappeared. In fact, I never met the man; he was found dead, the story goes, maybe that is what happened to your father, who knows.' Then she left it there, for us to digest and sip the tea and ponder over it. And we did just that, for days and years to come. Wondering if our father had disappeared and died somewhere.

Over the years, I watched her unpack dad's belongings one by one. And over the years they disappeared out of sight. The elephant tusk paraffin lamp that he brought from his trade union trip to Swaziland, the straw hat he bought in Lesotho that was woven in red and blue grass and beautifully thatched. Then his big brown leather belt with a silver buckle that he used to hit us and mother with, the screams of my mother becoming yells and his screams at us over the years. The binoculars, his golf clubs. Everything disappeared over time and so did my memories of him, till I planted a garden of spinach, tomatoes, and onions, and each morning when I watered it, I prayed over it for his return home.

We still sat on the floor to watch the television, no flinching no noise, just like we did when dad was there, we didn't run around the house, the orders were still obeyed, the rules, we were like child soldiers; the bed-making routine was observed every morning, followed by shoe polishing every evening in the stoep, looking at the moon and just wondering what planet my dad was on now, and which one his father was on.

The radio seemed like my only solace, every evening I listened to storytelling on my PP9 battery-powered Eveready Nomathotholo. Characters came to life, 'Gonondo omkhulu osabekayo', stories that a 14-year-old imagination identified with, stories of beautiful forests, animal sounds and happy places. The bright sunshine was also a charging dock, and I would leave my battery on the windowsill all day long, and then use it by night. The radio drama was an escape, into a world of imagination and in that world I belonged, I had a place. I knew then that I wanted to become a Storyteller and a writer.

I did have friends and places to visit and people to see, but to me there was more to life than going to church every Sunday, dressed-to-kill and singing the same hymns. There had to be more to it than polishing church pews and brass on a Saturday. I often wondered about 'the other side', the white people side. The side that we were not allowed to go on, where the signs clearly stated 'Whites Only'.

I often imagined about that side, where you would see

beautiful parks and children having ice cream on beautiful benches, they seemed to be in paradise. We only played Upuca (stone game with a hand drawn circle) or Umshinxi or Black Toti. Those were our childhood games, and such games kept us away from home and away from trouble. We definitely did not have beautiful parks with benches, we were lucky to even have Kool-Aid on a sunny day.

Mother worked and withered away between the old and the new. She could see the end of Apartheid was coming, we would hear rumours that Mandela was going to be freed. The anxiety came from the change that was coming, both in our home and from outside. The 'Whites Only' signs started to disappear, and soon enough, Mother took us out more often, she kind of softened. It was fun to get on a taxi to go to the Mall in Greenacres, it was there that I had my first ice cream, vanilla, on a cone draped in chocolate. I remember going to the cinema to watch *Coming to America*. I had never experienced such intensity in my life, such joy, such pleasure. I called it 'Byscop', that's what it was called from our side. Even though we ventured out more, we tried to make the divides disappear, like lines in the sand, the reality was harder, the mental divides were harder to erase, the dos and don'ts, the beatings, the harsh words, the stigma of Apartheid hanging on like a bad smell in the air.

I left South Africa in 2001. I left Mother, left places that still had signs and people who still believed that they were 'the chosen ones'. I left my newly found food, pizzas, ice creams, and newly discovered places like malls and cinemas. I wanted to find my paradise, a place where I could be a writer and storyteller. I wanted to find an audience. And sure enough, I found it in a place called Belfast. I soon learned a new language and culture. 'What about ya?' was now my new way of talking, and soon enough I had a daughter—a Millie. 'Oh Mummy, what have I done?' And now she asks me, 'Mummy, are we Black Catholics or Black Protestants?' Just when I thought I had left politics in South Africa.

There are no verandas here in Ireland, just Peace Walls. It is cold here… just like the people I had left behind. I miss Mother, and sometimes I often wonder what she would make of this new home I call Belfast.

ACKNOWLEDGEMENTS

Acknowledgments are due to the following publications in which versions of some of these poems have appeared: *Four x Four, Incubator, Of Mouth, View, Books Beyond Boundaries NI, Fortnight@50, Bangor Literary Journal, Community Arts Partnership* and *Affinity*.

I would like to thank Lisa Frank, John Walsh and Tríona Walsh for taking on a Xhosa woman who has a lot to say, dance and sing to. In these poems I do that.

The book is dedicated to Anesu Khanya, my Black Irish daughter, who had to endure years of prejudice, stereotypes and racism. 'Could you not have chosen anywhere else in the world?' she sometimes asks me. My reply has always been, 'This place chose me.' It chose us to pluck the seed of ignorance, in that we both became writers and poets that Ireland needed to hear and see.

I would like to thank Damian Smyth of the Arts Council of Northern Ireland. At some point the dream died and he revived it. Thanks also to Maria McManus, Viviana Fiorentino, Raquel McKee, Dr Carolann North, Dr Shelley Tracey, Moyra Donaldson, Roseleen Walsh, Aunty Liz Weir and Lisa Mooney.

Thank you to all the poets I ever performed with, too many to name, but your encouragement over the years has been a lifeline. I'm extremely grateful for the support from the Arts Council of Northern Ireland and to the organisations that I've been fortunate to work with over the years, including Quotidian, Building Communities Resources Centre, Terra Nova Productions, Macha Productions, Arts Ekta, Armstrong Storytelling Trust, Prime Cut Productions and Imagine Festival, Community Arts Partnership and the John Hewitt International Summer School.

NANDI JOLA is a South African born poet, storyteller and playwright, as well as a Smock Alley Theatre Rachel Baptiste 2022 Programme recipient. She was a creative writing facilitator for Ulster University Books Beyond Boundaries NI in 2021. Her one woman play 'The Journey' opened the International Literature Festival Dublin in October, 2020. She represented Northern Ireland at the Transpoesie Poetry Festival in 2021 and is a commissioned poet for Poetry Jukebox, Ambiguities, a James Joyce programme of the Centre Culturel Irlandais and Impermanence Way Archive Project 2022. She is studying for her MA in Poetry at Queen's University Belfast.